FIFTY WAYS TO PRACTICE WRITING

TIPS FOR ESL / EFL STUDENTS

DOROTHY ZEMACH

WAYZGOOSE PRESS

CONTENTS

How To Use This Book   1

PART I
PRACTICE, PRACTICE, PRACTICE

1. Make a daily habit   7
2. Use a picture   8
3. Keep a journal   9
4. Practice your handwriting   10
5. Dictation   11
6. Make a picture dictionary   12
7. Write out responses from textbook exercises   13
8. Translate   14
9. Send texts   15
10. Freewrite   16
11. Create a "writing environment"   18

PART II
INSPIRATION

12. Write holiday greeting cards   21
13. Write a bucket list   22
14. Write a letter to the editor   23
15. Write a thank-you letter   24
16. Write answers to questions   26
17. Experiment   27
18. Explain a process   28
19. Start a Postcard Club   29
20. Write directions   31
21. Describe a scene   32
22. Plan a trip   33

PART III
SKILLS AND STRATEGIES

23. Use new vocabulary — 37
24. Work on speed — 38
25. Paraphrase 1 — 39
26. Paraphrase 2 — 40
27. Practice notetaking and summarizing — 41
28. Learn about punctuation — 42
29. Write in different locations — 43
30. Increase your word variety — 44
31. Increase your sentence variety — 45
32. Change point of view — 47
33. Plan your writing — 49

PART IV
TYPING I: IMPROVING SKILLS

34. Free practice online — 53
35. Relax with a game — 54
36. Copy a paragraph from newspaper, book, or magazine — 55
37. Use social media in English — 56
38. Use Twitter in English — 57
39. Try tandem language learning or a keypal — 58

PART V
TYPING II: ADVANCED PRACTICE

40. Take shortcuts — 63
41. Format online — 64
42. Give up abbreviations — 66
43. Write online reviews — 67
44. Use a spellchecker — 68
45. Don't use a spellchecker — 69
46. Be very careful with grammar checkers — 70
47. Start a blog — 72
48. Join an online forum — 74
49. Try "Written? Kitten!" — 75
50. Try "Write or Die" — 76

Bonus tip!   78
Afterword   80

HOW TO USE THIS BOOK

It takes many hours to become proficient at anything—a sport, a hobby, a musical instrument, or a foreign language. Many thousands of hours, in fact! For a student of English, this can seem difficult to accomplish, especially if your only opportunity to study English is in the classroom.

This book will help you learn and practice writing in English, both inside and outside the classroom. If you are already taking English classes, some of the tips will help you get more out of your classes. If you're not taking English classes – and even if you are – other tips will give you ideas to try on your own. Not every idea will work for every student. That's why there are fifty. We feel sure that many of the ideas presented here will bring you results if you try them sincerely.

.   .   .

Here is a suggested method for using this book:

1) Read through all of the fifty tips without stopping.

2) Read through the tips again. Choose five or six that you think might work for you. Decide when you will try them, and for how long.

3) Try to choose different types of ideas: some for practicing fluency (such as journals or freewriting), some for practicing accuracy, with grammar or punctuation, some for handwriting, and some for typing. Also, choose some that you can practice with a friend or language learning partner, and some that you can do alone. For your convenience, the tips are divided into two main categories, *Writing* and *Typing*. The *Writing* suggestions can almost all be done both with paper and pencil and on a computer; the *Typing* suggestions are meant for use with a computer or tablet.

4) Each time you use one of the ways, make a note about how well it worked for you and why. Remember that most of the tips will work best if you practice them several times (or even make them a habit). Don't try a tip only once and decide it's no good for you. Give the tips you try a few chances, at least.

5) Every few weeks, read through the tips again, and choose some new ones. Discontinue using any methods that are not working for you.

The most important advice, though, is to actually *do* the suggestions you read about here. Wishing is not working. If you don't do the work, you won't see the results.

Finally, consider trying some of the other books in our *50 Ways to Practice* series. No one skill in English is really separate from the others. Speaking, listening, reading, writing, vocabulary, and grammar are all connected. Improving in one area will almost always bring improvements to other areas too.

PART I

PRACTICE, PRACTICE, PRACTICE

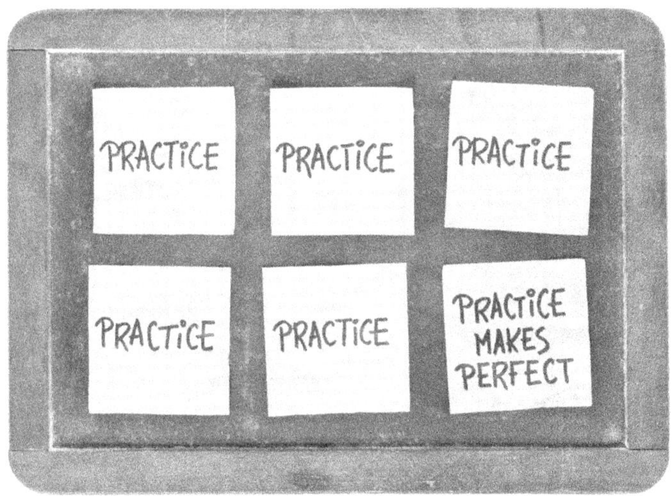

You probably already know the saying in English, "Practice makes perfect." That's not really true for writing—there isn't any such thing as "perfect writing." However, it is certainly true that practice will make you a lot better, and it will also make writing easier and more enjoyable.

In this section, you will find some tips on how to create a writing practice for yourself.

1

―――

MAKE A DAILY HABIT

Even a very short time practicing can help you improve—but you have to do it regularly.

Every day, write five sentences in English. You can use pen or pencil and paper, or you can type on the computer or even make notes on your phone.

If you write in the evening, you can write about what you did during the day. If you write in the morning, you can write about what you are going to do or what you plan/want to do. In this way, you can practice different verb tenses.

Why not write both in the morning and in the evening? Keep a notebook and pen or pencil by your bed.

USE A PICTURE

This is a wonderful technique for everyone from beginners to experts.

Find a picture in a magazine or online, and either describe what you see or write a short story about it. It can be a landscape, a person's face, an advertisement—anything that you can describe.

Check new vocabulary you need in a dictionary.

If you want to see your progress, paste or tape the picture into a notebook, and write underneath it. The next time you write, put a new picture on the next page, and so on. If you do this regularly, you will naturally start to write faster, and you'll also write more.

Soon you will have a portfolio of your writing. You can look back and see how much better you are now!

3

—————

KEEP A JOURNAL

Write a journal about any topic that interests you, or keep a diary about the things that happen to you. You can write on paper or on a wordprocessor. You can even keep a journal or diary online, private or public (see Tip #48 on blogs).

You don't have to write every day, but you should write several times a week. The more often you write, the faster your writing will improve.

You will also find it interesting in the future to go back and read your thoughts and experiences from the past.

4

PRACTICE YOUR HANDWRITING

Even native English speakers need this! If you are someone who spends a lot of time typing or texting, you might not have many chances to practice your handwriting.

The best way to improve your handwriting is—you guessed it—to practice regularly. Get a book of poems or find some online, and copy one each day into a notebook.

You could also copy a poem onto a postcard and send it to a friend or family member. That is a nice way to show someone you are thinking about them.

5
____

DICTATION

Work with a friend. Your friend reads a paragraph from an English book (or an article from a newspaper or online site) and you write it down.

When you're finished, check what you wrote against the original. Did you spell everything correctly? Did you punctuate everything correctly?

Then you read something for your friend to write.

If you do not have any friends who speak English, you can use the text-to-speech function of your phone or other device and ask it to "read" something to you. But be careful not to study the text in advance! Or you are not really taking dictation.

MAKE A PICTURE DICTIONARY

You can use this technique to learn vocabulary for a hobby (perhaps you like sewing or horseback riding) or the workplace (do you work in a factory or a store?), or you can make a dictionary for children or beginners.

You can print images that you find online, draw your own, or even take photos with your camera and make your dictionary an electronic document.

Label the pictures, and write two or three sentences about each picture. For example, you may want to write your own definition or an explanation of how an object is used.

You can also make an alphabet book: Find one picture that begins with A, then one that begins with B, and so on. Then read it to a child who is learning English.

7

WRITE OUT RESPONSES FROM TEXTBOOK EXERCISES

If you are taking an English class that uses a book with exercises, you can use that book for additional writing practice.

After class, go over questions that you answered by speaking (either one-sentence answers or longer answers), and this time, write your answers down. This will also help you practice vocabulary and grammar from that lesson.

If you are not taking an English class, you can still buy a textbook and use it in the same way. Make sure you get one at your level of English or even slightly below.

8

———

TRANSLATE

Choose a paragraph or two in your native language, and express it in English.

Some ideas might be easy to translate directly, and others might be more difficult. Generally, you cannot easily translate one word or even one sentence at a time. You will need to understand one *idea*, and then think about how to express that in English.

Check any new vocabulary in English in the dictionary. If there are grammatical structures you cannot translate, save these until you can ask a teacher or higher-level student to help you.

SEND TEXTS

Texting is a good way to practice because you usually have your phone with you almost all the time. You can take advantage of short amounts of time when you can't easily practice English in other ways—for example, when you are riding on the bus or waiting in an office for an appointment.

Find a friend who is also studying English. Agree to exchange text messages in English every day. It's okay if each text is only a few words or sentences.

If you can text someone whose English is better than yours, you can also learn some common abbreviations and texting language from them.

10

FREEWRITE

Write (you can also type) for five or ten minutes without stopping. Don't think too much – just write the first thoughts that come into your head. If you don't know a word in English, just write xxx or write it in your own language. Don't worry about making mistakes, and don't go back and erase or cross things out. Just write, write, write! This exercise will help with your speed and fluency.

If you can practice freewriting with a friend, you can choose ideas for each other. If you are practicing alone, get a box or a jar. Write topic ideas on little pieces of paper and put them into the jar. Then when it's time to freewrite, choose an idea without looking and write about whatever you find.

Here are fifteen ideas to get you started:

- rain

- stars

- something that makes me laugh

- babies

- a food I hate

- my ideal vacation

- things that annoy me

- a childhood friend

- mountains

- a goal for the future

- a good career

- telephones

- paper

- something I'm afraid of

- my favorite song

CREATE A "WRITING ENVIRONMENT"

Organize a space in your room or home where you can write comfortably.

Make sure your desk or table area is clear and that you have good lighting and a comfortable chair. Your feet should be able to rest flat on the floor.

Do you want to decorate your space? Perhaps a nice poster of a destination you would like to visit, or a vase of flowers, or a pretty scene.

Keep a dictionary, paper, pen, pencils, erasers, whatever you need close by.

Experiment to see if you write more easily with a little background music or in silence. Do you want a cup of coffee or tea?

Over time, you will be able to sit down in your writing environment and your mind will feel ready to write.

PART II

INSPIRATION

When you are taking a class at school, the teacher tells you what to write about. But what about when you are on your own? Then the ideas have to come from you! For some writers, finding ideas or inspiration is as hard as the actual writing.

In this section, then, you will find plenty of ideas for what to write about.

WRITE HOLIDAY GREETING CARDS

See if you can find paper greeting cards for any holiday that you or a friend celebrates. Then write a message in English, and mail the card at the appropriate time.

If you are not sure what expressions to use in English, check online. You can also write a regular message, though.

If you can't find paper cards, you can also send online cards; there are many sites that have free e-cards.

Or you can design and create your own paper cards!

WRITE A BUCKET LIST

Write a list of a number of things you want to learn, do, or experience before you die. (Note: The term "bucket list" refers to things you want to do before you "kick the bucket," or die.) Examples might be things like *Have a child, Visit Argentina, Learn to play the guitar.*

Every few months, check your bucket list again, and write sentences about each item to explain whether you have done it or haven't; and if you haven't, why not. For example, *I haven't had a child yet because I'm still not married. I visited Argentina last summer. I haven't learned to play the guitar yet because I haven't had time to take lessons.*

Then write a new bucket list by removing the things you've already done and things you've changed your mind about wanting to do.

WRITE A LETTER TO THE EDITOR

Read your local or regional newspaper (either in paper or online) or a national or international news article. Write a letter to the editor expressing your opinion about one of the issues they discussed.

Check the editorial page of the publication and read examples of letters that other people wrote. This will show you how long letters usually are, and what kind of writing style other people use.

Even if your letter is not published, you still get the writing practice!

15

———

WRITE A THANK-YOU LETTER

Think of someone who helped you or did something nice for you—such as a friend, a family member, a coach, or a teacher (but not one teaching a class you are currently taking; you don't want them to think you are just trying to get a better grade!).

Write a thank-you letter to that person and express your appreciation. Here are some useful phrases:

- *Thank you for (helping me to move to my new apartment).*
- *I really appreciate it.*
- *I am grateful that you (called me when I was sick).*
- *I really enjoyed (going to the park) with you.*
- *I want to thank you for (listening to me the other night).*

Write on paper with a pen in your nicest handwriting, and then mail it. You can also email thank-you letters, of course, but a handwritten one will seem more special.

WRITE ANSWERS TO QUESTIONS

Buy one of these books of questions, and regularly pick a question and write out the answer.

The simplest questions are in *4,000 Questions for Getting to Know Anyone and Everyone*, by Barbara Ann Kipfer.

Challenge yourself with more philosophical questions from *The Book of Questions*, by Gregory Stock or *If... (Questions For The Game of Life)*, by Evelyn McFarlane and James Sewell.

If you don't live in an area that has an English-language bookstore, you can order online from Book Depository, which has free worldwide shipping, or buy an ebook version.

17
———

EXPERIMENT

Try different kinds of writing. Write a funny story, a joke, a song, a sad story, your life story, a biography of your hero or favorite singer/actor, a poem, a letter, a video game review, a short play... anything!

Often when you try something completely new, you feel less pressure and can be more creative. You can choose to share your new writing with someone, or even keep it completely private.

Sometimes writers who wish to experiment create a *pen name*—that is, they use another name as the "author" of their new writing. Why not experiment with a pen name yourself? Choose a new name for a new kind of writer, and then, as that new person, write something new!

18

———

EXPLAIN A PROCESS

Choose a simple process that you understand well, such as making coffee or tea, uploading a photo to a social media site, mending a hole in a sock, tying a necktie, and so on.

Write out the instructions for a complete beginner. When you are finished, check your instructions to make sure you didn't leave any steps out.

If you feel ambitious, you can act out your instructions as you read them, film yourself, and upload your how-to video to YouTube, Instagram, or TikTok.

START A POSTCARD CLUB

Find some friends who are also studying English. It doesn't matter if they are in the same city as you or if they live far away. Agree to exchange postcards in English regularly (once a week, once every two weeks, etc.).

You will have fun selecting new pictures to send your friends. You can comment on the scene on the card, or just send a friendly message.

Remember to start and end your card appropriately: Write the date at the top, begin with *Dear* (your friend's name), and at the end write *Your friend* (or *best wishes*), and then sign your name at the very bottom.

There are even services that will turn your personal photos into postcards and mail them. One such service is Touchnote, online here:

https://touchnote.com/

You have to create an account and buy some credits. Then you can upload a photo, type out your message, enter your friend's address, and Touchnote will mail your card as an actual postcard.

You can buy an annual membership (good for people who want to send a lot of cards) or purchase individual credits (better for people who want to send just a few cards).

You can create both postcards and greeting cards.

WRITE DIRECTIONS

Imagine that you have to give instructions to someone about how to get from one place to another. For example:

- from the nearest train station or bus stop to your house
- from your house to your school or workplace
- from your house to the airport
- from your city to the beach

Directions can be simply how to walk somewhere—*go straight for two blocks, turn left, walk about half a kilometer,* etc. Or you could include public transportation directions: *Buy a train ticket to X. Make sure you take the local train. Transfer at X station to the Z line.*

Write out precise instructions. Save them—you might need to give them to someone someday!

21

DESCRIBE A SCENE

Watch a DVD or clip from YouTube and then summarize one scene in the movie. Use connecting words like *next*, *then*, *because*, *after*, *while*, and so on to connect your sentences and keep the story organized.

You can also just describe characters (looks and personality) or a place to practice descriptions.

A more advanced option is to then give your opinion about what you saw. You can comment on the story line, the quality of the acting, how the music made you feel, and so on.

PLAN A TRIP

Pick a city or a country that you would like to visit. Look up 10 vocabulary words that you will need to write about the trip.

Then write a paragraph for 15 minutes about what you would do in that city or country.

Check your spelling, grammar, and punctuation after you finish the paragraph. Were you able to use all of the ten words you looked up?

PART III

SKILLS AND STRATEGIES

Practice is wonderful, but it's important to work on the mechanics of writing too, sometimes—saying what you want to say accurately and correctly.

This section has advice and strategies for improving the quality of your writing.

23

USE NEW VOCABULARY

"Use it or lose it!"

During one week, write down some new English words that you encounter that you think would be useful. Check a dictionary for meaning and example sentences. If you need more example sentences, search for your word online and see how others use it.

Then when you write in your journal or diary (see tip #3), or do some freewriting (see tip #10), try to use as many of the week's words as you can.

24

———

WORK ON SPEED

Decide how many words, lines, or paragraphs you are going to write before you start writing. Time yourself, and see how long it takes.

If you do this once a week for a month or two, you will probably notice that your writing speed improves.

It's good to do this with both handwriting (especially if you are used to using your phone all the time) and typing on a keyboard. However, "thumb typing" on your phone is still writing, and it's useful to be able to do that quickly in English too.

There are further suggestions for increasing typing speed in Section IV.

PARAPHRASE 1

To *paraphrase* something means to say the same thing in another way.

You can do this by changing words to synonyms, or by changing the sentence structure.

Here is an example:

1. *It's important to buy a car that is energy-efficient.*
2. You should get a car that uses fuel efficiently.
3. It's crucial to purchase an energy-efficient automobile.

Do you see how sentences 2 and 3 mean the same thing as #1? Sentence #2 is a little less formal, and sentence #3 is a little more formal.

Rewrite three sentences in your textbook using different words, or by saying the same idea in a different ways.

PARAPHRASE 2

For a longer challenge, read a news story of a few paragraphs. Read it several times until you can remember the main ideas and some details.

Then, without looking, write the same story in your own words (don't just write sentences that you were able to memorize).

When you are finished, compare your version to the original. Were all the facts correct? Did you include the most important ideas? Did you tell the story in a different way (different grammar, different vocabulary)?

Paraphrasing is an important academic skill, and one that takes a lot of practice.

PRACTICE NOTETAKING AND SUMMARIZING

Listen to a short lecture on a topic interesting to you – check TED talks, for instance. (You can find them on YouTube, too.)

Take notes (of course in English!) while you listen. If necessary, you can listen more than once.

Some lectures are even subtitled in English, but it's best to enable this option at the checking stage, not when you are first trying to take notes.

If a lecture is difficult, just listen to it the first time, and try taking notes the second time.

After you have finished taking notes, write up the notes in paragraph form. Imagine you are answering a question such as "What is the main idea of the lecture?" or "What does the lecturer want listeners to know or do?"

LEARN ABOUT PUNCTUATION

There are a lot of rules about English punctuation (using commas, semicolons, quotation marks, and so on). You cannot learn them all at one time.

Buy a style guide or grammar book, or research punctuation online.

Study one area at a time. Make one month "comma month," for example, or "semicolon month."

Read through the rules a few times, and then a few days later, read them again. Pay attention to these marks you are studying when you are reading. When you write, make an effort to use the "mark of the month" correctly. Check the style guide if you are not sure or if you forget something.

WRITE IN DIFFERENT LOCATIONS

This is my best tip for overcoming "writer's block"—when you have an assignment due but can't think of anything to say.

When I am blocked, I change locations. If I'm sitting on the sofa with my laptop, I move to the dining room table. If I'm at home, I move to a coffeeshop (this book was written in at least three different cafés as well as my house). Even if you only move to the other side of a table, you might find that changing your position helps you get new ideas.

If you cannot change positions (for example, you're working on a desktop computer that can't be moved), then refresh yourself by going for a five-minute walk.

INCREASE YOUR WORD VARIETY

Most writers tend to use some words over and over again. Look back at some of your writing, and circle words you seem to use a lot (not words like *the* and *to*, of course, but words like *good* and *though*).

Find some words with a similar meaning—either ask a friend or teacher or use a *thesaurus* (there are free online thesauruses).

Then when you write, make an effort to use your new words to add variety and interest to your writing.

INCREASE YOUR SENTENCE VARIETY

Most English sentences follow the pattern of subject + verb, sometimes with an object or an adverbial phrase after the verb. However, many of these adverbial phrases (which can be single words, short expressions, or prepositional phrases) can be moved to other positions in the sentence.

For example, you can write

I wake up at seven every morning.

or

Every morning, I wake up at seven.

The basic meaning is the same, although the feeling is a little different. Generally in English, the part of the sentence that comes first is the most important.

You can also change the position of many sentence connectors. For example, you can write

I like typing. However, I'm not very fast at it.

(or *I like typing; however, I'm not very fast at it.*)

I like typing. I'm not very fast at it, however.

When you read, pay attention to these types of variations in sentence patterns, and use them when you write too. Also make sure your writing has both short and long sentences.

CHANGE POINT OF VIEW

Write a few paragraphs about your own life—for an example, a trip you took once or some short incident. Write in "first person" first—using *I*, *me*, *my*, *mine*, and so on.

Then, rewrite the same story in third person, as if someone else was writing about you; use *he* or *she*, *his* or *her*, etc.

This sounds like a simple exercise, but it can be tricky, too. You have to change verb forms as well as pronouns and adjectives. It's easy to make mistakes with these when you are writing quickly, so this exercise will improve your accuracy.

Compare:

> I got up late this morning and made my bed before
> I called my mother. She said I need to make a
> dental appointment, so this afternoon I'm going to
> do that.

He got up ate this morning and made hissed before he called his mother. She said he needs to make a dental appointment, so this afternoon he's going to do that.

PLAN YOUR WRITING

Many writers, even experienced ones, try to skip the "planning" stage of longer papers, which makes them very difficult to write.

Before you start writing an essay or research paper, make sure you have brainstormed ideas and organized them, so you know what you want to say and in what order you want to say it.

You don't necessarily need to write a formal outline, but you should at least write a list of ideas in the correct order. That way you won't leave out any important information.

Even though it might seem like brainstorming ideas and writing out your organization takes up more time, it will actually *save* you time to do this important "pre-writing" work because your first draft will be easier to write. Also, your first draft will be better, so you will save time on revising and writing a second draft.

PART IV

TYPING I: IMPROVING SKILLS

These days, being able to type quickly and accurately is an important writing skill. You will need to be a good typist if you plan to take tests such as the iBT TOEFL test, where you have to type timed essays, and also if you plan to work in an office or other work situation where you have to type letters and other business documents.

If you don't have a computer or easy access to a computer, find an old keyboard somewhere – doesn't matter if it's broken! – and use that to practice with. It's true that you won't be able to check your accuracy, but you can still practice, and that's better than nothing. You're building muscles and learning patterns with your fingers. You can even practice on a piece of paper with letters drawn on it, but a real keyboard, even one that doesn't work, will feel more realistic and is better.

FREE PRACTICE ONLINE

Try a site such as http://www.freetypinggame.net that has a variety of games, lessons, and practice tests.

https://www.typingclub.com/ has free lessons in touch typing.

You can also search for terms like "free typing lessons" or "free typing practice" to find other sites.

Note that different countries have different keyboards—that is, an American English keyboard looks just a little different from a French keyboard, even if the letters both languages use are the same. If you are not using a standard English keyboard (sometimes called a QWERTY keyboard, because Q-W-E-R-T-Y are the top five letters on the left-hand side), you might need to search for lessons specifically for your country's keyboard.

RELAX WITH A GAME

If you have online access, play free typing games such as Typer Shark—search for the name to find a site that works for you.

https://www.typinggames.zone/ is a site that has games mostly for children—but even a game for children will work for adults as well.

Games start at a very easy beginner level, and keep pushing you to type faster while still being accurate.

If you can't get online often, consider buying a copy of the game.

36

COPY A PARAGRAPH FROM NEWSPAPER, BOOK, OR MAGAZINE

Good typists can do what we call "touch typing"—that is, they can type without looking at the keys at all, because their fingers know where all the letters are.

To increase your typing speed and accuracy, and learn to touch type, choose something to copy. Just a paragraph or two is enough at first.

Make sure you don't look at the keyboard while you type! Only look at what you are copying.

Then check to see how many mistakes you made. If you made a lot, try it again, but more slowly.

Practice this once a day if you can, or at least a few times a week.

USE SOCIAL MEDIA IN ENGLISH

Even if you don't have many (or any) friends who speak English, you can still post your status updates and thoughts in both English and your native language on social media accounts such as Facebook, Instagram, and LinkedIn.

By posting in both languages, everyone can understand what you want to say, and you have a great chance to practice writing in English. Just a few sentences isn't hard, and you probably won't need to look up many new words. Also, if you have bilingual status updates, you will attract other English speakers to connect with you, and therefore provide more practice.

To practice both writing and speaking, you could write out a short paragraph and then video yourself reading it to post on Instagram or TikTok.

USE TWITTER IN ENGLISH

Only 140 characters at a time – you can do that! That's just a few short sentences.

Open a Twitter account and try to use it at least once a day. Follow friends and other people who seem interesting (many celebrities have Twitter accounts) and you will see the kinds of messages people write.

But even if you don't have any followers at first, you can still write your messages and just ... send them out there. The practice is good for you!

TRY TANDEM LANGUAGE LEARNING OR A KEYPAL

Practice English while you help someone else practice your language by finding a language study partner. For example, you could meet someone in Australia who wants to learn Spanish, while you in Bolivia want to practice English. You each send emails to each other and help each other. There are a few ways to do this. Here is a common way:

1. You each write a letter in the language you are studying. So, in the case above, A (in Australia) writes a letter to Spanish to B (in Bolivia); and at the same time, B writes a letter in English to A.
2. Then, you each answer the other person's letter (in your native language)—so, B will write back to A in Spanish, and A will write back to B in English.

This means you will have two "chains" of letters going, each one in a different language. That way you are both practicing and teaching at the same time,

You can also find another person who is studying English, and has a level similar to yours. Then you each email in English.

In the past, there were several large websites and free services that helped people find tandem language partners and keypals. However, many of them were put out of business by social media.

Here is one site that was still active when this book was published (2023):

https://www.mylanguageexchange.com/

More advanced students can also use this site for conversation and discussion partners.

These days, you can also find a partner or a keypad on your favorite social media site. It might take a few tries to find someone who has similar goals, and who is serious about practicing language.

PART V

TYPING II: ADVANCED PRACTICE

Even when you feel pretty comfortable typing on an English keyboard, you can always improve your skills.

This section has some more advanced tips for typists who can already easily find all the letters on the keyboard.

Of course, as you are practicing your typing, you are also practicing many other writing skills.

TAKE SHORTCUTS

Learn these keyboard shortcuts to help increase your typing speed:

PC: *save* (control + s), *copy* (control + c), *cut* (control + x), *paste* (control + v), *undo* (control + z), *redo* (control + y), *print* (control + p).

Macintosh: *save* (command + s), *copy* (command + c), *cut* (command + x), *paste* (command + v), *undo* (command + z), *redo* (command + y), *print* (command + p).

"Control + something" means that you hold down the control (or command) key, which is to the left of your space bar, and while you are holding it down, you also press the letter. Note: These commands are for an English system and English keyboard. If you are using a system or keyboard for a different language, these might not work.

FORMAT ONLINE

Learn these basic html codes, and use them when you comment on a website or post to your own blog. In the examples below, the first tag begins your special formatting, and the second one ends it.

italics <i> </i>

bold <b> </b>

Put these tags around the word or sentence that you want to change. For example, if you want the word "typing" to be bold in this sentence:

I love typing.

then you would write it like this:

I love <b> typing </b>.

Then it will look like this:

> I love **typing**.

Experiment a bit on sites that allow html formatting. If there are other effects you want (different colors, different letter sizes), you can search for more html codes online. Learn a few at a time, and have fun with them.

GIVE UP ABBREVIATIONS

If you already text some people in English, challenge yourself to a week of no texting abbreviations or sentence fragments. (You might want to let your friends know what you are doing!)

It's true that fluent speakers of English as well as native speakers do use abbreviations, such as *u* for *you*, *b4* for *before*, or *KWIM* for *(Do you) know what I mean.*

However, if you want to practice your writing, you should also get used to full forms and standard English, so those patterns become habits for you too.

Note that most native English speakers do not use texting abbreviations in email or formal letters, only on the phone.

WRITE ONLINE REVIEWS

There are many places online where people review products and services, such as books on Amazon, Apple, and Goodreads; hotels, flights, and restaurants on Trip Advisor; and just about anything on epinions.

If you have read a book, stayed in a hotel, bought a camera, rented a car, used a computer, liked a dress or a shirt ... write a review so that other potential customers know what you thought.

Give your overall opinion (did you like it, not like it, or a bit of both?) and then give a few reasons to support your opinion. You are welcome to review this book!

USE A SPELLCHECKER

Don't think that just because "it's online" or "it's only social media" that good spelling doesn't matter.

Words that are spelled wrong are harder for someone else to read. So if you are writing something that is going to be read by someone else, make it as correct as you can.

Many email programs and word-processing programs and Internet browsers contain automatic spellcheckers, though you may need to turn them on.

If you are typing on a forum or some other place online that does not have a spellchecker, then write your message first in a document on your computer, check it with the spellchecker, and then copy and paste the corrected message.

DON'T USE A SPELLCHECKER

If you have a spellchecker automatically correcting your mistakes, you might become less aware of what correct spelling is.

Challenge yourself to type a page with the spellchecker turned off. Then read your page. Underline any words that you know how to spell, but just typed incorrectly. Double underline any words that you think might be spelled wrong.

Then turn on your spellchecker and check your page.

If there were words you didn't know how to spell, make flashcards with them and test yourself for about a week until you can spell them confidently.

This is especially useful for advice for anyone planning to take a test like the TOEFL iBT, which does not allow spellcheckers.

46

BE VERY CAREFUL WITH GRAMMAR
CHECKERS

The grammar checker that comes with most popular word-processing programs is a mixed blessing. It might tell you some things are wrong when they are not. It might miss some things that are wrong. Some grammar checkers will mark things like passive constructions (*The Eiffel Tower was built in 1889*) or sentence fragments and imply that they are always "wrong" or "bad" – and they are not. A grammar checker can find subject-verb agreement problems, such as

He speak too fast. X

but then it might also tell you this is a subject-verb agreement error, and it's not:

The people in this movie speak too fast. √

That is, the grammar checker will decide that "movie" is

singular, and so it should be "movie speaks." However, the subject of speak is people, so the sentence is correct. A grammar checker simply cannot think like a person.

However, a grammar checker can also find things like words you accidentally repeated and extra spaces between words. Unless you are very confident about your English, I suggest using a grammar checker only to find things such as these.

START A BLOG

There are many free online blogs that are not hard to use, such as WordPress and Blogger. Choose one that looks good to you, and just start experimenting!

You can create a blog about one topic (your university, your family, a trip you took, your hobby, a story in the news that is interesting to you) or you can use it as an online diary.

You can choose your level of privacy, too: For example, you can set the blog so that no one can read it except you. You can set it so that only people you 'invite' can read what you write. Or you can make it completely public. You can change this setting at any time if you want to do things differently.

Read instructions for your blogging platform and learn how to include photos (use your own photos, though— don't just take photos from online sites, because they might be copyrighted) and links to other sites.

You can also explore other people's blogs, and leave comments—another good way to practice writing!

JOIN AN ONLINE FORUM

These days you can find online forums for all kinds of subjects—people who enjoy a certain sport or hobby, fans of different celebrities, people who want to lose weight, people from the same religion, just about anything.

One popular site is http://reddit.com. You can search there for discussions about all kinds of topics.

Join a forum, and take part in the online conversations. You will be most successful if you spend a few weeks "lurking"—that is, just reading and not posting—until you understand the personality and habits of that writing community.

Be warned that bad manners and strong language are common in many online forums. If you find a forum unpleasant, though, you can simply stop using it.

TRY "WRITTEN? KITTEN!"

Do you want a fun way to encourage yourself to write longer passages? Try "Written? Kitten!" The site can be found here:

https://writtenkitten.co/

Simply start typing on the screen. After you write 100 words, the program will automatically reward you with a picture of a kitten.

You can change the settings so that the pictures come after every 200 words, 500 words, or even 1000 words. The site tells you what your word count is as you go along. This is a very good way to get used to knowing how long it takes you to write a certain number of words, which is useful for some exams.

Don't like cats? Don't worry—you can also choose puppies or bunnies.

TRY "WRITE OR DIE"

How brave are you? "Write or Die" is a program that forces you to keep typing steadily. You can use the program online at this address:

https://v2.writeordie.com/

or you can download a copy (for purchase) for your computer, phone, or iPad (it's not very expensive).

You can then use it in three modes, from easy to very strict. You start typing ... and if you stop, it will either remind you (nicest mode), play an annoying noise (medium level), or —at the strictest level—start erasing what you have written!

You can set the amount of time you can rest before the consequences begin. The program will also count your words and time your writing session.

Begin with 5 or 1-minute sessions, and build up to 15 or 20 minutes. You can save what you have written and copy it into a regular word-processing program later.

Try this program with freewriting or journal writing, not with important school assignments!

BONUS TIP!

<u>READ</u>

Yes, reading is one of the best things you can do to improve your writing. There are several reasons for this.

You will expose yourself to vocabulary and grammar used naturally, as well as different writing styles. You will see how other writers explain their ideas, and what words and structures they use.

Most people prefer to read for pleasure, so choose some things that you enjoy. It really doesn't matter what you read—a poem, a short story, a magazine article, the subtitles on a TV show, song lyrics, a novel, a how-to guide, a video game manual, a recipe... it's all English, and it's all helpful.

However, if you are studying English for any kind of written exam or for the workplace, it's also important to read the kinds of things that you will be asked to write.

AFTERWORD

Learning another language is never fast, but the *Fifty Ways to Practice* series will speed things up by showing you how to practice more efficiently and effectively, both inside and outside the classroom. It is useful for beginning through advanced levels. The *Fifty Ways to Practice* series offers short, practical guides to different areas of English language study for motivated students.

Note: We have priced these *Fifty Ways to Practice* guides very cheaply, because we want education and learning to be available to as many people as possible. However, our authors are highly qualified professionals who work hard to create these books. If these books are useful to you, please recommend them to your friends—but please do not share them freely. Our authors will continue to write excellent and cheap books for you if they make a little money. That way, we all win. Thank you for your support!

If you have comments or suggestions (such as ideas for future books that you would find useful), feel free to contact the publisher at editor@wayzgoosepress.com, check out the offerings on our publishing website at http://wayzgoosepress.com, or join us on Facebook.

To be notified about the release of new *50 Ways* titles, as well as other new titles and special contests, events, and sales from Wayzgoose Press, please sign up for our mailing list. (We send email infrequently, and you can unsubscribe at any time.)

www.ingramcontent.com/pod-product-compliance
Lightning Source LLC
Chambersburg PA
CBHW072048150726
47996CB00015B/2159